Giant Moray Eel

GIANTS of the **OCEAN**

Anita Yasuda

MEDIA ENHANCED BOOKS

AV2 BY WEIGL™

ADDED VALUE • AUDIO VISUAL

www.av2books.com

AV² provides enriched content that supplements and complements this book. Weigl's AV² books strive to create inspired learning and engage young minds in a total learning experience.

Your AV² Media Enhanced books come alive with...

Go to **www.av2books.com,** and enter this book's unique code.

BOOK CODE

E296507

AV² by Weigl brings you media enhanced books that support active learning.

Audio
Listen to sections of the book read aloud.

Video
Watch informative video clips.

Embedded Weblinks
Gain additional information for research.

Try This!
Complete activities and hands-on experiments.

Key Words
Study vocabulary, and complete a matching word activity.

Quizzes
Test your knowledge.

Slide Show
View images and captions, and prepare a presentation.

... and much, much more!

Published by AV2 by Weigl
350 5th Avenue, 59th Floor, New York, NY 10118
Website: www.av2books.com   www.weigl.com

Library of Congress Cataloging-in-Publication Data

Yasuda, Anita, author.
 Giant moray eel / Anita Yasuda.
    pages cm. – (Giants of the ocean)
 Includes index.
 ISBN 978-1-4896-1090-4 (hardcover : alk. paper) – ISBN 978-1-4896-1091-1 (softcover : alk. paper) –
 ISBN 978-1-4896-1092-8 – ISBN 978-1-4896-1093-5
 1. Morays–Juvenile literature. I. Title.
 QL638.M875Y37 2015
 597.43–dc23

                        2014004320

Printed in the United States of America in North Mankato, Minnesota
1 2 3 4 5 6 7 8 9 0 18 17 16 15 14

032014
WEP150314

Senior Editor: Heather Kissock
Design: Mandy Christiansen

Weigl acknowledges Getty Images as the primary image supplier for this title.

Contents

Meet the Giant Moray Eel

The giant moray eel is an incredible fish. It looks like a snake with its long, thick body. The giant moray is the largest eel in the world. It is known for its strength and its sharp, snappy teeth.

When a giant moray eel is young, its body is tan with large black spots. As the eel gets older, the spots change into leopard-like markings. This spotted pattern helps it blend into its watery home.

Unlike most fish, the giant moray eel does not have scales. Instead, its skin is smooth and coated with slime called mucus. This mucus helps the moray to slide over rocks and other rough surfaces without scratching itself. The mucus also protects the eel from **bacteria** and **parasites**.

Nestled in its rocky home, the giant moray is most often seen opening its mouth and flashing its teeth. While this looks ferocious, the eel is not threatening the fish around it. The giant moray opens its mouth to pump water over its **gills**.

Moray eels have small eyes and cannot see very well. They use their superb sense of smell to find food.

All About Giant Moray Eels

All eels belong to the Anguilliformes order. *Anguilla* is the Latin word for "eel," and *forma* means "shape." The Anguilliformes order is large, with more than 600 **species** of eels. This order is divided into 19 families. Moray eels belong to the Muraenidae family.

Where Giant Moray Eels Live

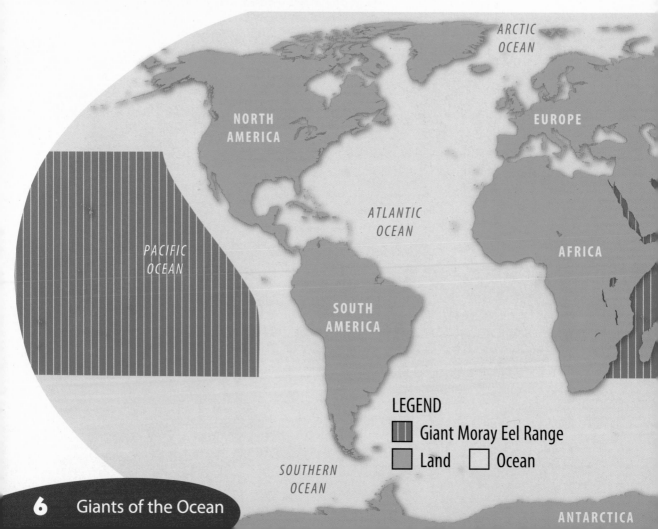

ARCTIC OCEAN

NORTH AMERICA

EUROPE

PACIFIC OCEAN

ATLANTIC OCEAN

AFRICA

SOUTH AMERICA

LEGEND
- Giant Moray Eel Range
- Land
- Ocean

SOUTHERN OCEAN

ANTARCTICA

There are about 200 kinds of moray eels. Morays have thin bodies with large heads and powerful jaws. They come in many color patterns and sizes. Snyder's moray is the smallest, at 4.5 inches (11.5 centimeters) long. Slender giant morays are the longest at 13 feet (4 meters) in length.

The giant moray eel is the largest member of this family. Some giant morays weigh as much as 66 pounds (30 kilograms).

├─ Up to 13 feet (3 m) long ─┤

Can live for about
30 years

Also called the
Java moray

A solitary animal that prefers to **live alone**

Classifying Moray Eels

ORDER
Anguilliformes

FAMILY
Muraenidae

GENUS
Gymnothorax

SPECIES
Javanicus

ASIA

PACIFIC OCEAN

INDIAN OCEAN

AUSTRALIA

N

The Home of Giant Moray Eels

Giant moray eels live in the warm, tropical waters of the Indian and Pacific Oceans. They are found as far north as Japan's Ryukyu Islands and as far south as New Caledonia and the Austral Islands of Oceania. They make their homes in lagoons and **coral reefs**. Some moray eels stay in the deep ocean slopes off Indonesia. Young moray eels sometimes hide in intertidal zones. These are areas just off shore where the tide is always rising and falling.

Despite their size, giant moray eels are designed to fit into the tightest of spaces. During the day, they tuck themselves into holes along the reefs and hide. Like all morays, the giant moray eel is **nocturnal**. At dusk, giant morays leave their homes to hunt. The reefs are full of **prey,** including shrimps.

Some giant morays find hiding places in **wrecks of old ships**, in **spongy seaweed**, and in **underwater caves**.

Holes and cracks in coral reefs provide excellent resting and hunting grounds for giant moray eels.

Features of Giant Moray Eels

Giant moray eels have developed many **adaptations** that help them survive in reefs. Unlike most fish, they do not have side fins. This makes it possible for them to swim with ease through tight cracks and narrow openings.

TEETH
The giant moray has very long needle like teeth, which it uses to rip apart its prey. The teeth point inwards, making it difficult for prey to escape the eel's bite.

POWERFUL JAWS
A giant moray has a large mouth with two sets of strong jaws. When prey is caught, the jaws lock onto it. The prey cannot break loose due to the strong hold.

DORSAL and CAUDAL FINS

Giant morays have a long, muscular fin running along their backs. Called the dorsal fin, it keeps the eel stable when it is moving through the water. The dorsal fin joins with the eel's tail, or caudal, fin. This makes it look as if the eel has only one fin.

BODY

The giant moray has a long and thick body. It propels itself through the water by undulating its body from side to side. The eel's long spine bends easily, allowing it to twist its body into different positions. This helps the giant moray fit into small crevices.

Diet of Giant Moray Eels

Moray eels are **carnivores**, feeding mostly on fish, squid, and octopuses. Different species of moray feed in different ways. Some lie in wait. Their patterned skin allows them to blend into their surroundings and surprise prey. Other eels are hunters who chase after their dinner. Giant moray eels are hunters. They catch their prey as they swim through coral reefs. They feed mostly on bony fish, shrimps, and crabs.

A giant moray can eat a fish up to **3 feet** (1 m) long.

Fish open their mouths wide to suck in prey, but moray eels cannot do this. When a giant moray feeds, it relies on its second set of jaws. This extra set is located in the back of its throat. The eel's front jaw grabs hold of prey like a fork. While the first set of jaws is holding the food, the second set of jaws pulls the prey into the eel's stomach.

The giant moray swallows small fish whole. It uses its teeth to crush shelled animals. Once the food is crushed, moray eels dump what they cannot digest. This is why they are known as messy eaters.

Cleaner shrimp help moray eels stay healthy by picking debris out of their teeth.

Life Cycle of Giant Moray Eels

Giant morays usually live alone. They only come together to **mate**. This usually happens in summer when the water is warmer.

Females lay more than 10,000 eggs at a time. Male morays then **fertilize** the eggs. The adult morays do not look after the eggs. Instead, the fertilized eggs float off into the ocean.

The eggs that survive will float until they hatch into **larvae**. Giant moray larvae are flat, thin, and almost clear. They are shaped like tiny leaves. Larvae eat decaying plants and animals on the ocean surface.

Larvae can drift for eight or nine months in the ocean, where there are fewer predators to eat them. Over time, the larvae change into small juvenile eels. As they mature, their bodies become thicker and longer.

The gender of a moray eel can change. Some morays begin life as males and later change into females.

The Cycle

Moray Eels Spawn
They signal interest by gaping their mouths.

Female Lays Eggs
The male and female separate after **spawning**.

Eggs Hatch into Larvae
They are about 3 inches (7 cm) in length.

Larvae Become Juvenile Eels
The larva develops into a young eel in eight months. When the eel is stronger, it swims down to the reefs to live and feed.

Juveniles Becomes Adult Eels
A giant moray can live up to 36 years.

History of Giant Moray Eels

Eels have been on Earth for a long time. Scientists believe that ancestors of the eel lived during the Cretaceous period, 144 to 65 million years ago. Over time, their **pelvic fins** disappeared, and their dorsal and caudal fins joined together.

In 1859, Pieter Bleeker was the first to identify the giant moray eel. Bleeker was a Dutch military doctor and **naturalist** who worked in the Dutch East Indies, an area now known as Indonesia. Bleeker collected hundreds of fish. He published his findings in scientific magazines.

The giant moray eel's scientific name is *Gymnothorax javanicus. Gymno* is Greek, for "bare," and *thorax* means "chest," which describes the moray eel's smooth body. *Javanicus* is Latin for "Java," where the giant eel was seen. Today, scientists are still discovering new facts about the giant moray.

A giant moray's territory can cover a few hundred yards (m) or **several miles** (kilometers).

Although the giant moray eel looks fierce, it is a shy animal. It is aggressive only when it feels threatened.

Encounters with Giant Moray Eels

For centuries, sailors feared the giant moray eel. They believed it to be a sea monster. The ancient Romans, however, built special fishponds near the sea to house them and served them at banquets.

Today, through careful study, people have come to learn more about these creatures and respect them. Divers and scientists work together to study giant morays. In the past 10 years, much has been learned about these incredible creatures.

One important area of study is how giant moray eels hunt. In 2006, Professor Redouan Bshary of Switzerland was studying grouper fish. He noticed some odd behavior in the group he was tracking. One grouper seemed to be waking up a moray. Further study revealed that giant moray eels and groupers were hunting together in the Red Sea.

Video recordings showed the two animals seeking each other out to hunt. The grouper would approach the giant moray and shake its head. This seemed to invite the eel to hunt. The two animals would then begin swimming together, helping each other find prey.

Groupers and eels **do not share** their catch. Whoever grabs the prey eats it **all**.

Unlike the giant moray, the grouper's body is not flexible enough to chase prey into crevices in the reef.

Conservation

The giant moray eel population is considered healthy. The fish is currently in no danger of becoming **extinct**. However, it still faces challenges in its environment. The main threat to its lifestyle comes from humans.

Climate change and pollution are affecting coral reefs around the world. The reefs are changing as a result of rising temperatures and water content. Organisms living within these **habitats** rely on certain conditions. As the habitats change, these organisms will begin to decline. The first organisms to disappear tend to be the less common species. This would include the giant moray. Scientists are urging that steps be taken to protect these habitats and the organisms within them to ensure they stay healthy in the future.

Myths and Legends

Sina and the Eel

Long ago, there was a beautiful girl. Her name was Sina. She lived on an island called Samoa. Word spread of Sina's beauty throughout the islands of the Pacific.

One day, King Tuifiti of Fiji heard about Sina. He knew that he had to go to the island to meet her. To get there quickly, he decided to turn himself into an eel. He then swam and swam until he reached Samoa.

As it happened, Sina was swimming in the ocean that day. Tuifiti swam up to her. Sina liked the eel and decided to keep it for a pet. She did not know it was Tuifiti.

First, Sina kept her new pet in a bowl. When it outgrew the bowl, she put it in a pool. The eel would not stop growing, and Sina became frightened of it.

She ran away to a neighboring village, but the eel found her. The eel approached Sina and told her who he was and why he followed her. The journey had taken much from him, however, and he soon died.

When Sina buried him, a beautiful tree grew on the site. This was the first coconut tree.

Test Your Knowledge

There are many different moray eel species in the oceans. The activity below will help you learn more about different types of morays. You will need two blank sheets of paper and a pencil or pen.

Materials

Two sheets of Paper   Pencil

1 Using this book and other resources, read about different species of moray eels and their characteristics.

2 Now, using what you have learned, draw a picture of four different moray eel species on the first sheet of paper. Label your drawings with the name of each type of moray eel.

3 Across the top of the second sheet of paper, write down the species of the moray eels you drew. Then, in point form, write down how these species are similar and different from one another.

Quiz

1 What do most fish have on their bodies that moray eels do not?

2 What helps giant moray eels to slide over rough surfaces?

3 What family do giant moray eels belong to?

4 Where do giant moray eels hide during the day?

5 How many sets of jaws does a giant moray have?

6 After eels hatch from eggs, what are they called?

7 What do eel larvae eat in the ocean?

8 What animal picks food from the teeth of a giant moray eel?

9 In what year was the giant moray eel identified as a separate species?

10 How many eggs does a female giant moray lay?

Answers:
1. Scales 2. Mucus
3. Muraenidae family 4. Reefs
5. 2 6. Larvae 7. Decaying plants
and animals 8. Cleaner shrimp
9. 1859 10. More than 10,000

Key Words

adaptations: changes in plants and animals that make them better able to live in a particular place or situation

bacteria: tiny organisms that cannot be seen with the eye alone

carnivores: animals that eat other animals

coral reefs: groups of underwater plants and animals

extinct: no longer living on Earth

fertilize: to put male cells inside an egg to reproduce

gills: respiratory organ in fish

habitats: the natural environments of organisms

larvae: the earliest stage of development for many types of animals before becoming adults

mate: to reproduce

naturalist: a person who studies nature

nocturnal: active at night

parasites: animals that live on another animal and use it for food or shelter

pelvic fins: a pair of fins on the underside of a fish's body

prey: an animal hunted as food

spawning: laying a group of eggs in water

species: a group of creatures that have many features in common

Index

Log on to www.av2books.com

AV² by Weigl brings you media enhanced books that support active learning. Go to www.av2books.com, and enter the special code found on page 2 of this book. You will gain access to enriched and enhanced content that supplements and complements this book. Content includes video, audio, weblinks, quizzes, a slide show, and activities.

AV² Online Navigation

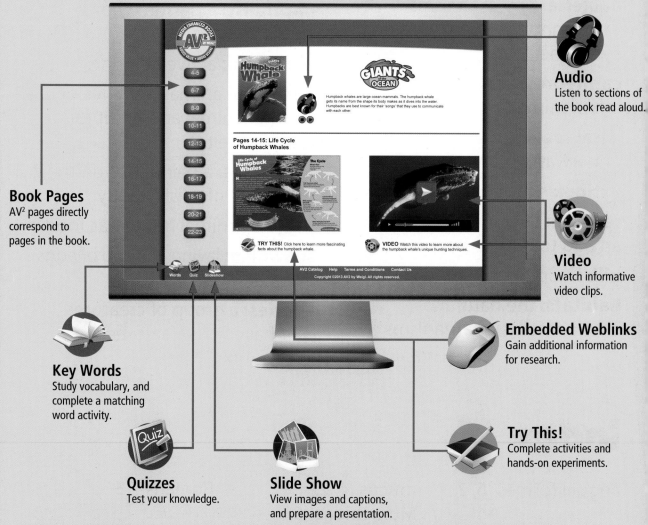

Book Pages
AV² pages directly correspond to pages in the book.

Audio
Listen to sections of the book read aloud.

Video
Watch informative video clips.

Key Words
Study vocabulary, and complete a matching word activity.

Embedded Weblinks
Gain additional information for research.

Quizzes
Test your knowledge.

Slide Show
View images and captions, and prepare a presentation.

Try This!
Complete activities and hands-on experiments.

AV² was built to bridge the gap between print and digital. We encourage you to tell us what you like and what you want to see in the future.

Sign up to be an AV² Ambassador at www.av2books.com/ambassador.